Cornerstones of Freedo

DUE

Arlington National Cemetery

R. Conrad Stein

CHILDRENS PRESS®
CHICAGO

Library of Congress Cataloging-in-Publication Data

Stein, R. Conrad.
    Arlington National Cemetery / by R. Conrad Stein.
      p. cm.–(Cornerstones of freedom)
    ISBN 0-516-06625-0
    1. Arlington National Cemetery (VA)—Juvenile literature.
[1. Arlington National Cemetery (VA)]
I. Title. II. Series.
F234.A7S72 1995
975.5'295—dc20   95-6307
                       CIP
                       AC

For U.S. Marines, the February 1945 assault on Iwo Jima was the bloodiest battle of World War II. Japanese troops defending the tiny island fought with a desperate fury that shocked even those Marines who were veterans of other Pacific battles. After four days of savage combat on Iwo Jima, a group of Marines reached the top of Mount Suribachi, Iwo Jima's highest point. Amid the smoke and roar of battle, six men raised an American flag on a tall pole while a photographer named Joe Rosenthal snapped a picture. That picture inspired Americans at home and became the most famous photograph taken during World War II.

Joe Rosenthal's famous photograph of Marines raising the American flag at Iwo Jima

Ira Hayes

One of the Mount Suribachi flag raisers was twenty-two-year-old Ira Hayes. He was a Pima Indian, born on a reservation in Arizona. After fighting at Iwo Jima, Hayes returned to the United States a war hero. A painfully shy man, Hayes could not adjust to his sudden fame. One night in 1955 he got drunk, passed out, and died. Ira Hayes now rests at the Arlington National Cemetery in Arlington, Virginia. Some people who knew him believe that finally, in the quiet grounds of the cemetery, he found peace. Two other men who were in the historic picture—Rene Gagnon and Michael Strank —also rest at Arlington.

The U.S. Marine Corps War Memorial reproduces the Joe Rosenthal Iwo Jima photograph. The memorial is near Arlington National Cemetery.

Joe Louis worked to raise soldier morale during World War II with his boxing exhibitions. He was a hero to many African Americans.

Joe Louis was not a war hero, but during the 1930s and 1940s, he was almost as famous as the president of the United States. Louis was the boxing heavyweight champion of the world from 1937 to 1949. Nicknamed "the Brown Bomber," he had a lightning-quick left hand and a thunderous right. Many experts still say he was the best prizefighter in history. An African American, he was especially idolized by the nation's blacks.

Joe Louis's gravesite at Arlington

Shortly after the U.S. entered World War II, Joe Louis enlisted in the army as a private. He traveled from camp to camp giving boxing exhibitions to soldiers, thereby helping to improve morale. Some people criticized Joe Louis's efforts. In the 1940s, African Americans in many states were not allowed in the same movie theaters, restaurants, or public schools as whites. Even the army in which Louis served was segregated, with blacks and whites kept in separate units. A critic once asked Louis why he was willing to help a nation that treated his people so poorly. Louis answered, "I don't think Mr. Hitler would do any better." Joe Louis died in 1981, and he now rests at Arlington National Cemetery, where there is no segregation.

There are more than 250,000 graves at Arlington. Fully three-quarters of them are marked by simple, government-issued headstones, which are curved at the top and rise about knee-high to the average man. Seemingly endless rows of these white headstones stretch over rolling acres at Arlington. The rows resemble soldiers standing at attention. Though most of the gravestones are identical, each represents the life of a man or a woman and consequently tells an individual, and often heroic, story.

There are more than 250,000 graves at Arlington National Cemetery.

Arlington is one of 114 national cemeteries maintained by the United States government. The major purpose of a national cemetery is to serve as a burial place for veterans of the country's armed forces. Situated across the Potomac River from Washington, D.C., Arlington has long been close to many Americans' hearts. It is the final home of citizens from all backgrounds. Buried there are ex-presidents as well as former slaves. More than four million people visit the cemetery every year. A walk over its grassy hills is a walk through American history.

Mary Ann Randolph Custis

The land we now know as Arlington National Cemetery was purchased in 1778 by John Parke Custis. Mr. Custis had a famous mother—Martha Washington, wife of the nation's first president. John Custis was Martha Washington's son by her first marriage. Custis died while serving in George Washington's army in the Revolutionary War. After he died, the land was passed on to his son, George Washington Parke Custis.

The younger Custis named the land Arlington, after a family estate that once stood on the Virginia shore. He married and raised a beautiful daughter, Mary Ann Randolph Custis. The family lived in a mansion, called Arlington House, which was built on the property's highest hill.

George Washington Parke Custis, Martha Washington's grandson

Robert E. Lee (1807–1870) was commander of the Confederate Army through most of the Civil War. Lee's Virginia plantation eventually became Arlington National Cemetery.

In 1831, Mary Ann married a young army lieutenant, Robert E. Lee. The marriage brought another Virginia family, as old and as honored as the Washingtons, into the Arlington story. Lee's father was "Light Horse Harry" Lee, a dashing commander who led a cavalry unit in the Revolutionary War. For almost thirty years, Robert E. Lee and his wife, Mary Ann, lived happily on the Arlington plantation, which then spread over 1,100 acres.

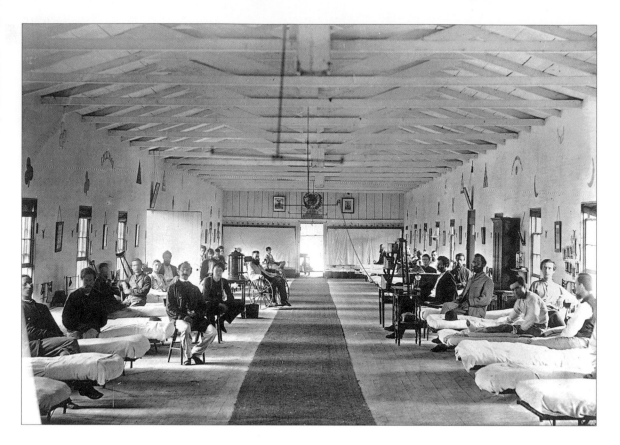

A Washington, D.C., hospital during the Civil War

In 1861, the Lee family and the nation were ripped apart by the Civil War. The South's desire to continue owning slaves was the root cause of the terrible war. It raged for four years and cost more lives than any other conflict in American history.

Though he was a southerner, Robert E. Lee hated slavery. He once wrote, "Slavery is a moral and political evil in any society, a greater evil to the white man than to the black." Still, Lee felt deep emotional ties to Virginia and to the southern states. He left his home and his family to command the Confederate Army. Lee never again returned to Arlington, the home he loved.

President Lincoln (center) and Union officers

Throughout the Civil War, Arlington was in the hands of Union (northern) troops. Just across the Potomac River from Arlington, the city of Washington served as an immense Union Army camp.

At the height of the conflict, some two thousand wounded and ill Union soldiers were shipped each week from battlegrounds to hospitals in the nation's capital. Many of those stricken troops died. Nearby graveyards quickly became full. So in the spring of 1864, President Abraham Lincoln asked Quartermaster General Montgomery Meigs to establish a new national cemetery. Meigs selected Arlington as the site.

Montgomery Meigs

A Civil War memorial at Arlington National Cemetery

Many historians believe that Meigs, who despised Robert E. Lee, chose Arlington just to deprive the Lee family of its estate. In a cruel irony of war, Meigs's own son, Lieutenant John Rodgers Meigs, was killed in action in October 1864. He was buried in what was once Mrs. Lee's rose garden.

When the Civil War ended in 1865, there were already 18,000 graves at Arlington. Many of the dead belonged to the South's defeated Confederate Army. Today, the old Confederate grave sites are easy to pick out because they have pointed, rather than curved, stones. An Arlington legend says the stones were designed by southerners with points on top to prevent Yankees (northerners) from sitting on them.

Confederate soldiers' gravestones in Arlington have pointed, not curved, tops.

Arlington soon became the nation's most prestigious military cemetery. The remains of some soldiers who fought in previous wars were moved from other cemeteries and re-buried at Arlington. The cemetery now holds veterans of all American wars from the American Revolution of the 1700s to the Persian Gulf War of 1992. Some of the honored dead at Arlington were generals or admirals whose deaths commanded newspaper headlines. Others were common soldiers who fell on the battlefield, their deaths unnoticed by anyone except their families and friends.

More than four million people visit Arlington every year.

John Clem

Oliver Wendell Holmes

One grave holds John Clem, a Civil War veteran known as the "Drummer Boy of Chickamauga." Clem ran away from home at age ten and served as a drummer boy for the Union. After the war, he stayed in the army and climbed to the rank of brigadier general. At age sixty-five, Clem tried to re-enlist so he could fight in World War I, but he was turned down because he was too old.

Another Civil War soldier resting at Arlington is Oliver Wendell Holmes. His fame came not on the battlefield, but later, as one of the greatest justices ever to serve on the United States Supreme Court. As a young army officer, Holmes was fighting in a battle near Washington when he noticed that this skirmish had a famous observer. Standing tall above a rampart was President Abraham Lincoln, who watched the combat while bullets whistled dangerously close to his head. Holmes cried out, "Get down, you fool!" Finally, Lincoln ducked. He later said to Holmes, "Young man, I'm glad you know how to talk to a civilian."

Abner Doubleday is also buried at Arlington. Doubleday was the Union general in charge of Fort Sumter when it was fired upon by Confederate ships. But Doubleday's claim to fame is that for generations, he was believed to be the inventor of baseball. This event was supposed to have happened at Cooperstown,

Abner Doubleday

New York, in 1839, when Doubleday was a cadet in training at the nearby West Point Military Academy. More than a century later, baseball experts have proven this story to be a myth.

Historians believe the Spanish-American War, fought in 1898, helped to ease the bitterness that inflamed the country during the great Civil War. In the brief Spanish-American War, men of the northern and the southern states fought side by side, displaying a harmony that surprised their fathers, who still remembered the past conflict. A monument honoring Spanish-American War veterans was erected at Arlington in 1902. The monument was dedicated by that conflict's most celebrated veteran—President Theodore Roosevelt. Another memorial stands at Arlington honoring the many American women who served as nurses and died in the Spanish-American War.

Theodore Roosevelt (center, raised sword) was a military hero in the Spanish-American War. He later became president.

John J. Pershing

Few conflicts in history were as terrible as World War I, in which poison gas, machine guns, and rapid-fire artillery killed infantrymen in ghastly numbers. Commanding the American forces in that conflict was John J. Pershing. After the United States and its allies claimed victory in the war, a grateful Congress gave Pershing the title General of the Armies. It was a rank so rare that it had been held previously only by George Washington. Some people whispered that Pershing, though a splendid leader, was also an arrogant man who was unable to talk to his troops. But before he died in 1948, he requested his grave at Arlington be marked with a simple, government-issued stone, and that he be buried in a spot surrounded by the common soldiers he had commanded. In a grave near General Pershing's, his grandson is buried—Lt. Richard Pershing was killed in Vietnam in 1968.

America entered World War II when the Japanese bombed Pearl Harbor, Hawaii, on

General Pershing's burial ceremony at Arlington

December 7, 1941. Just four months after that attack, Jimmie Doolittle, who now lies at Arlington, led a flight of sixteen two-engine bombers on a daring raid against Japan. The huge planes had to take off from the pitching deck of an aircraft carrier in the middle of the Pacific Ocean and fly hundreds of miles over enemy-held waters to their target. For his bravery, Doolittle won the Congressional Medal of Honor, the nation's highest award.

The most decorated American soldier of World War II was a baby-faced Texas farm boy named Audie Murphy. Firing a machine gun mounted on a burned-out tank, Murphy once stopped an attack by some 250 German infantrymen. Though he was hailed as the nation's bravest soldier, the army was not Murphy's first choice. He had tried to enlist in the Marines, but he was turned down because he was too short. In 1971, Murphy was killed in an airplane crash and was buried at Arlington.

Audie Murphy

World War II hero Jimmie Doolittle, who is buried at Arlington

Marguerite Higgins was a news reporter who covered the Korean War. She is considered one of the most important American journalists of the century.

The Korean War of 1950–53 is often called the "Forgotten War." While it was being fought, it was largely ignored by the people at home, and it was later given scant mention in most history books. Reporting on the war for *Life* magazine was correspondent Marguerite Higgins, the only female correspondent near the front when the war began. Higgins's important role in the war was alerting the army and the public to the fact that the American soldiers' antitank weapons were outdated and ineffective against the giant North Korean tanks. Higgins now rests at Arlington. Korean War veterans hail her as a lone voice reminding Americans of the Forgotten War raging in a faraway land.

Not since the Civil War has a conflict divided the nation as bitterly as did the Vietnam War, fought in the 1960s and early 1970s. During that time, pro- and antiwar Americans argued and clashed on college campuses and on city streets. Antiwar protesters raged against the actions of the U.S. government, which was sending thousands of American troops to fight the communist forces of North Vietnam. Meanwhile, the American men and women in Vietnam attempted to do their duties, even if they did not understand the confusing politics behind the struggle.

In an emotional 1984 ceremony, Vietnam War veterans salute the remains of the Vietnam War's Unknown Soldier.

One dedicated Vietnam serviceman was air force officer Daniel "Chappie" James, Jr., who died in 1978 and was buried at Arlington. An African American, James joined the army air force in 1943, when the armed forces were still segregated. Overcoming prejudice, he became an officer and a splendid pilot. In Vietnam, he flew seventy-eight combat missions. After the war, James was promoted to four-star general, the first African American to achieve that rank.

In a 1972 ceremony, Daniel "Chappie" James is pinned with stars by his son (left) and wife (right). He became a four-star general, making him the first African American to achieve that rank in the history of the U.S. Air Force.

Left: Widow of a fallen Persian Gulf War soldier is presented with a folded American flag.

Below: This statue is an Arlington memorial to nurses who have served in the U.S. armed forces.

In the late 1990s, tensions between the United States and the Iraqi government reached a breaking point when Iraq invaded Kuwait, an ally of the United States. President George Bush ordered more than a half-million American troops to the Persian Gulf to repel the invading Iraqi forces. Partaking in the fury of this desert war was helicopter pilot Maria Rossi of New Jersey. Even though she knew she would have to fly in treacherous weather, Rossi volunteered for a difficult mission in March 1991. Early into the flight, her Chinook helicopter crashed, killing her and the crew she commanded. Inscribed on her headstone at Arlington is the message: "First Female Combat Commander to Fly in Battle." On the reverse side a plaque says, "May our men and women stand strong and equal."

The Apollo I *(left) and* Challenger *(right) crews*

The American effort to conquer outer space was not a war, but the crews manning space capsules faced the same perils as did combat soldiers. In 1967, all three men aboard *Apollo I* were killed when a fire swept through their craft while it was still on the ground. Two *Apollo I* crew members—Virgil Grissom and Roger Chaffee—were buried at Arlington, while the third—Edward White—was laid to rest at West Point. The men of *Apollo I* were part of a brave team of astronauts. Three of their crewmates eventually reached the moon in 1969.

Another tragedy struck the space program in January 1986, when the spacecraft *Challenger* exploded seventy-two seconds into its flight. All seven people aboard were killed, including Christa McAuliffe, a grade-school teacher who was to give classes via satellite television while in space. McAuliffe had described her space shuttle mission as "the ultimate field trip." A monument honoring the *Challenger* crew now stands at Arlington.

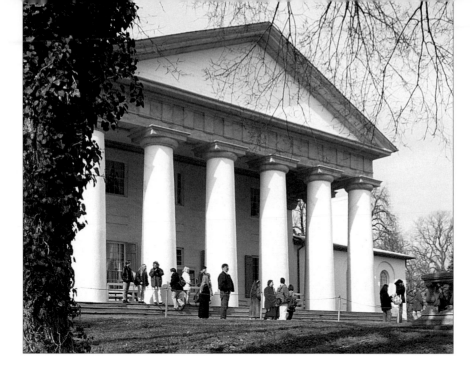

Built in 1817, Arlington House (left) stands on a high hill in Arlington National Cemetery. The house overlooks the Lincoln Memorial, the Reflecting Pool, and the Washington Monument in Washington, D.C.

Standing on a high hill in the center of Arlington National Cemetery is Arlington House. Many of its rooms have been stocked with period furniture to make them look as they did in 1861, when Robert E. Lee went to war. The front entrance to Arlington House presents a magnificent view of several Washington, D.C., landmarks. The city was planned and laid out in the late 1790s by Pierre Charles L'Enfant, a French architect hired by George Washington. In a remarkably forward-looking boast, L'Enfant told Washington he intended to design a capital so splendid it would serve "not for thirteen states, but for fifty." L'Enfant's grave stands in front of Arlington House, from which there is a grand vista of the city he helped to create.

Pierre Charles L'Enfant's grave

Schoolchildren visit the Eternal Flame that honors John F. Kennedy.

John F. Kennedy

Below Arlington House burns the Eternal Flame, which marks the grave of John F. Kennedy, the thirty-fifth president of the United States. Kennedy took office in 1961. He was young, vigorous, handsome, and he had the extraordinary ability to reach out to people and fill them with hope. As president, he once visited Arlington and found it so peaceful he said, "I could stay here forever." On November 22, 1963, Kennedy was struck down by an assassin's bullet in Dallas, Texas. After the cruel murder, a sense of shock paralyzed the country. Today, all Americans who lived through that time can recall exactly where they were and what they were doing when the terrible, unbelievable news came from Dallas.

In his 1961 inaugural address, Kennedy promised that his presidency "...will light our country and all who serve it, and the glow from that fire can truly light the world."

It is no wonder his grave is symbolized by the Eternal Flame.

Near John F. Kennedy lies his brother, Robert Kennedy, whose grave is marked by a simple white cross. Robert had picked up John's banner and was running for president in the 1968 campaign. On June 6, Robert Kennedy was also murdered by an assassin. At the Arlington funeral, his brother, Edward, said, "Some men see things as they are and ask, 'Why?' He saw things that never were and asked, 'Why not?'"

The newest grave at the Kennedy plot belongs to Jacqueline Kennedy Onassis (the widow of John F. Kennedy), who died in 1994. Americans will never forget the dignity she displayed during her husband's funeral. Dressed in black, with her children at her side, she marched in the procession showing a quiet courage which gave people strength during a period of confusion and fear. Jacqueline Kennedy's memory rings proudly at Arlington, shrine of heroes.

Robert Kennedy

John F. Kennedy, Jr. (kneeling), at the 1994 funeral of his mother, Jacqueline Kennedy Onassis

OTHER FAMOUS AMERICANS BURIED AT ARLINGTON NATIONAL CEMETERY

Omar Bradley
(1893–1981)
Popular World War II general who commanded Allied forces in Europe—the largest army ever assembled under the American flag

William Jennings Bryan
(1860–1925)
Famous orator, congressman, and leader of the Democratic Party from the 1890s through World War I; argued against lawyer Clarence Darrow in the famous Scopes "monkey trial" of 1925

Matthew Henson
(1867–1955)
African-American explorer who was the only American to accompany Robert Peary on the first successful expedition to the North Pole

George Marshall
(1880–1959)
American military general who was chief of staff for all American armed forces in World War II; later, as secretary of state, devised the "Marshall Plan," a program of American aid to help European economies recover after the war

Robert E. Peary
(1856–1920)
Former sailor in the U.S. Navy who later led a 1909 expedition that was the first to reach the North Pole

Walter Reed
(1851–1902)
Medical officer in the Spanish-American War who performed important experiments to discover the causes and cures of typhoid fever and yellow fever

Hyman G. Rickover
(1900–1986)
Naval officer who worked on designing the U.S.S. *Nautilus,* the first nuclear-powered submarine

William Howard Taft
(1857–1930)
Twenty-seventh president of the United States (1909–1913); the only president other than John F. Kennedy buried at Arlington

Earl Warren
(1891–1974)
Chief justice of the Supreme Court from 1953 to 1969; wrote the Court's 1954 opinion that outlawed racial segregation in public schools; also chaired the 1964 committee that produced the Warren Report, an investigation into President Kennedy's assassination.

A sentry is kept on duty at the Tomb of the Unknowns at all times.

One of the most moving experiences offered at Arlington is a visit to the Tomb of the Unknowns. Practically every war produces "unknowns"—soldiers whose bodies are so disfigured by bullets, bombs, or fire that they cannot be identified. In 1921, the remains of one such soldier, killed in World War I, were taken from a graveyard in France and re-buried at Arlington under a gleaming white sarcophagus bearing the words: HERE RESTS IN HONORED GLORY AN AMERICAN SOLDIER KNOWN BUT TO GOD.

The Unknown Soldier, being no one, could be anyone. Therefore, all the families who had lost a loved one whose remains could not be identified could worship at the grave of this unknown who represented all unknowns. In 1958, unknowns from World War II and Korea were buried at the site. An unknown from the Vietnam War was interred there in 1984.

Playing "Taps" at an Arlington funeral

The Tomb of the Unknowns is guarded by members of the Third Army Infantry, called "The Old Guard." During the day, an Old Guard sentinel marches twenty-one steps in front of the tomb, then stops and stares at the grave site for twenty-one seconds. This solemn ritual, watched by hundreds of silent tourists, is the equivalent of a twenty-one-gun military salute.

Flags almost always fly at half-mast at Arlington National Cemetery. In the distance, it is common to hear the lonesome refrain of a bugle sounding "Taps." About fifteen funerals are conducted on the grounds each day. Until the mid-1960s, anyone who had served honorably in the American armed forces and his or her spouse could be buried at Arlington. But available grave sites in the 612-acre cemetery grounds became scarce, and now burials require special approval.

Applicants who won medals in war or who were career members of the armed forces are given special consideration.

Across the Potomac River from the cemetery spreads the bustling, noisy city of Washington, D.C. Arlington, by contrast, is an island of tranquillity. Although the grounds are crowded with tourists during visiting hours, most guests are quiet, respectful of the dead. Private automobiles are not allowed in the cemetery. People walking amid the long rows of headstones tend to think silent thoughts of heroes, history, and the wastefulness of war. Many tourists ponder lines of poetry. One poem, written by a little-known poet named Theodore O'Hara, is an Arlington favorite. Its words are etched on plaques throughout the grounds:

> *On fame's eternal camping ground*
> *Their silent tents are spread*
> *And glory guards with solemn round*
> *The bivouac of the dead.*

GLOSSARY

bivouac – a temporary shelter for soldiers in a war

Confederate Army – the army of the South in the Civil War

Fort Sumter – Union Army fort where the first fighting of the Civil War took place

inter – to bury the body, or remains, of a dead person

Lincoln Memorial – monument in Washington, D.C., that honors President Abraham Lincoln

inter

plantation – a large farm

Reflecting Pool – a long, narrow body of water in Washington, D.C., that sits between the Washington Monument and the Lincoln Memorial

sarcophagus – a stone coffin

segregated – to be separated by race; a bus, school, restroom, or other facility where some races or religions are not permitted

Tomb of the Unknowns – monument at Arlington honoring soldiers killed in war whose bodies could not be identified

Union Army – the army of the North in the Civil War

Tomb of the Unknowns

West Point – the military academy where army personnel go to school

TIMELINE

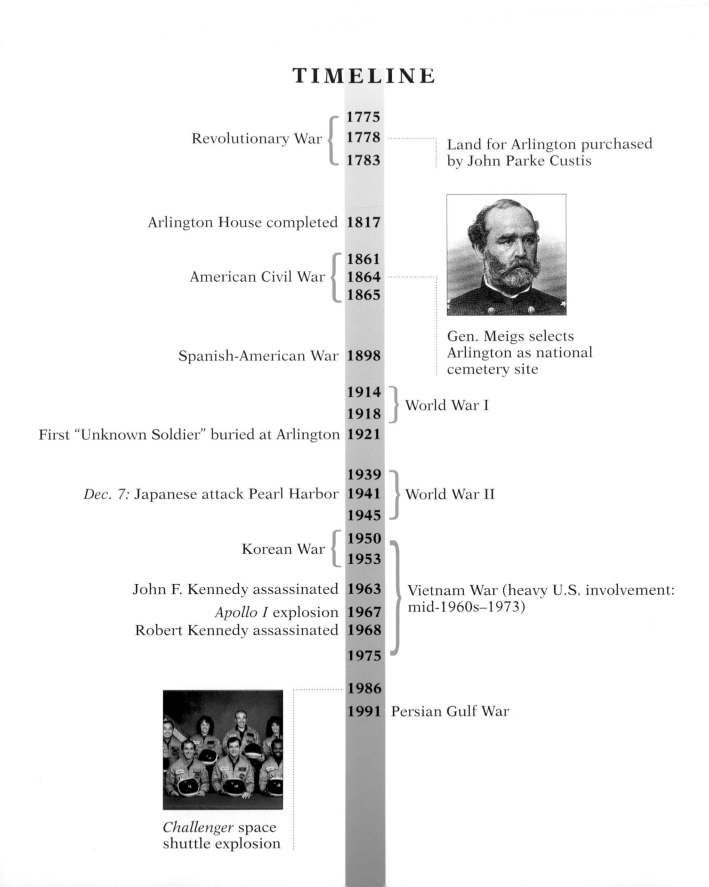

	1775
Revolutionary War	**1778** ········· Land for Arlington purchased
	1783 by John Parke Custis
Arlington House completed	**1817**
	1861
American Civil War	**1864**
	1865
Spanish-American War	**1898**
	1914 World War I
	1918
First "Unknown Soldier" buried at Arlington	**1921**
	1939
Dec. 7: Japanese attack Pearl Harbor	**1941** World War II
	1945
	1950
Korean War	**1953**
John F. Kennedy assassinated	**1963** Vietnam War (heavy U.S. involvement:
Apollo I explosion	**1967** mid-1960s–1973)
Robert Kennedy assassinated	**1968**
	1975
	1986
	1991 Persian Gulf War

Gen. Meigs selects Arlington as national cemetery site

Challenger space shuttle explosion

INDEX *(Boldface page numbers indicate illustrations.)*

PHOTO CREDITS

Cover, ©Mae Scanlan; 1, UPI/Bettmann; 2, 3, 4 (side bar), AP/Wide World; 4, ©Gene Ahrens; 5 (top), AP/Wide World; 5 (side bar), ©Dave Forbert; 6, ©P. Amranand/SuperStock; 7, AP/Wide World; 8 (both pictures), 9, 10, 11 (side bar), Bettmann Archive; 11 (top), UPI/Bettmann; 12 (both photos), ©Dave Forbert; 13, UPI/Bettmann; 14 (both photos), 15 (bottom), Bettmann Archive; 15 (side bar), UPI/Bettmann; 16 (side bar), AP/Wide World; 16 (bottom), Bettmann Archive; 17 (both photos), 18, UPI/Bettmann; 19, 20, AP/Wide World; 21 (top), UPI/Bettmann; 21 (side bar), ©Mae Scanlan; 22 (left), UPI/Bettmann; 22 (right), Jack Novak/SuperStock; 23 (top), ©Dave Forbert; 23 (right), ©Cameramann International, Ltd.; 24 (top), UPI/Bettmann; 24 (side bar), SuperStock; 25 (side bar), UPI/Bettmann; 25 (bottom), Reuters/Bettmann; 26 (background), ©Mae Scanlan; 27, ©M. Kazmers/SharkSong/Dembinsky Photo Associates; 28, UPI/Bettmann; 29, ©David Harvey/SuperStock; 30 (top), Bettmann Archive; 30 (bottom), ©M. Kazmers/SharkSong/Dembinsky Photo Associates; 31 (top), Bettmann Archive; 31 (bottom), Jack Novak/SuperStock

STAFF

Project Editor: Mark Friedman
Design & Electronic Composition: TJS Design
Photo Editor: Jan Izzo
Intern: Amy Vivio
Cornerstones of Freedom Logo: David Cunningham

ABOUT THE AUTHOR

R. Conrad Stein was born and grew up in Chicago. After serving in the Marine Corps, he attended the University of Illinois and received a degree in history. He is the author of many books for young readers, including several dozen in the Childrens Press Cornerstones of Freedom series. Mr. Stein lives in Chicago with his wife and their daughter, Janna.

    Over the years, Mr. Stein has visited Arlington National Cemetery several times. To prepare for this book, he made a special visit there, spent extra time on the grounds, and spoke to the cemetery's historian, Mr. Thomas Sherlock. The author wishes to thank Mr. Sherlock for his kind assistance.